Mass in B Minor

in Full Score

From the Bach-Gesellschaft Edition

Johann Sebastian Bach

DOVER PUBLICATIONS, INC.
Mineola, New York

Copyright

Bibliographical Note

This Dover publication, first published in 1998, is a republication of Volume (Year) 6 (1856), *Messe (H moll)*, edited by Julius Rietz, of the set *Johann Sebastian Bach's Werke*, originally published by the Bach-Gesellschaft in Leipzig. Lists of contents and instrumentation as well as translations of the Latin texts are newly added.

International Standard Book Number: 0–486–40417-X

Manufactured in the United States of America
Dover Publications, Inc., 31 East 2nd Street, Mineola, N.Y. 11501

CONTENTS

INSTRUMENTATION

2 Flutes [Flauto traverso]
3 Oboes (Oboe I, II = Oboe d'amore I, II)
2 Bassoons [Fagotti]

Horn (D) [Corno da caccia]
3 Trumpets (D) [Tromba]

Timpani

Violin Solo
Violins I, II
Violas
Cellos

Continuo (In *Sanctus*: Cello, Violone, Bassoon, Organ)

2 Solo Sopranos
Solo Alto
Solo Tenor
Solo Bass

Soprano I, II
Alto I, II
Tenor I, II
Bass I, II

TEXTS AND TRANSLATIONS

Kyrie

Kyrie eleison.
Christe eleison.
Kyrie eleison.

Gloria

Gloria in excelsis Deo, et in terra pax hominibus bonae voluntatis. Laudamus te, benedicimus te, adoramus te, glorificamus te. Gratias agimus tibi propter magnam gloriam tuam. Domine Deus, Rex coelestis, Deus Pater omnipotens. Domine Fili unigenite, Jesu Christe altissime. Domine Deus, Agnus Dei, Filius Patris. Qui tollis peccata mundi, miserere nobis. Qui tollis peccata mundi, suscipe deprecationem nostram. Qui sedes ad dexteram Patris, miserere nobis. Quoniam tu solus sanctus, tu solus Dominus, tu solus altissimus, Jesu Christe, cum Sancto Spiritu, in gloria Dei Patris. Amen.

Credo [Symbolum Nicenum]

Credo in unum Deum, Patrem omnipotentem, factorem coeli et terrae, visibilium omnium et invisibilium. Et in unum Dominum Jesum Christum, Filium Dei unigenitum, et ex Patre natum ante omnia secula. Deum de Deo, lumen de lumine, Deum verum de Deo vero. Genitum, non factum, consubstantialem Patri, per quem omnia facta sunt. Qui propter nos homines, et propter nostram salutem descendit de coelis. Et incarnatus est de Spiritu Sancto ex Maria Virgine; et homo factus est. Crucifixus etiam pro nobis sub Pontio Pilato, passus et sepultus est. Et resurrexit tertia die, secundum Scripturas. Et ascendit in coelum, sedet ad dexteram Dei Patris. Et iterum venturus est cum gloria judicare vivos et mortuos; cujus regni non erit finis. Et in Spiritum Sanctum, Dominum et vivificantem, qui ex Patre Filioque procedit, qui cum Patre et Filio simul adoratur et conglorificatur, qui locutus est per Prophetas. Et unam sanctam catholicam et apostolicam Ecclesiam. Confiteor unum baptisma in remissionem peccatorum. Et expecto resurrectionem mortuorum, et vitam venturi seculi. Amen.

Sanctus (Osanna, Benedictus)

Sanctus, sanctus, sanctus, Dominus Deus Sabaoth. Pleni sunt coeli et terra gloria ejus. Osanna in excelsis. Benedictus qui venit in nomine Domini. Osanna in excelsis.

Agnus Dei

Agnus Dei qui tollis peccata mundi, miserere nobis.
Agnus Dei qui tollis peccata mundi, miserere nobis.
[Agnus Dei qui tollis peccata mundi,] dona nobis pacem.

Kyrie

Lord, have mercy on us.
Christ, have mercy on us.
Lord, have mercy on us.

Gloria

Glory to God in the highest, and on earth peace to men of good will. We praise thee, we bless thee, we adore thee, we glorify thee. We give thee thanks for thy great glory. Lord God, heavenly king, God the Father almighty. Lord, the only-begotten Son, Jesus Christ most high. Lord God, Lamb of God, Son of the Father. Thou who takest away the sins of the world, have mercy upon us. Thou who takest away the sins of the world, receive our prayer. Thou who sittest at the right hand of the Father, have mercy upon us. For thou alone art holy, thou alone art the Lord, thou alone, Jesus Christ, with the Holy Ghost, art most high in the glory of God the Father. Amen.

Credo [Nicene Creed]

I believe in one God, the Father almighty, maker of heaven and earth, and of all things visible and invisible. And in one Lord Jesus Christ, the only-begotten Son of God, born of the Father before all ages. God of God, light of light, true God of true God. Begotten, not made, consubstantial with the Father, by whom all things were made. Who for us men and for our salvation came down from heaven. And was incarnate by the Holy Ghost of the Virgin Mary; and was made man. He was crucified also for us under Pontius Pilate, suffered and was buried. And on the third day he rose again, according to the Scriptures. And ascended into heaven, and sitteth at the right hand of God the Father. And he shall come again with glory to judge the living and the dead; and his kingdom shall have no end. And [I believe] in the Holy Ghost, the Lord and giver of life, who proceedeth from the Father and the Son, who together with the Father and the Son is worshiped and glorified; who hath spoken by the prophets. And [I believe] in one holy catholic and apostolic Church. I confess one baptism for the remission of sins. And I await the resurrection of the dead, and the life of the world to come. Amen.

Sanctus (Osanna, Benedictus)

Holy, holy, holy, Lord God of hosts. Heaven and earth are full of thy glory. Hosanna in the highest. Blessed is he that cometh in the name of the Lord. Hosanna in the highest.

Agnus Dei

Lamb of God, who takest away the sins of the world, have mercy on us. Lamb of God, who takest away the sins of the world, have mercy on us. [Lamb of God, who takest away the sins of the world,] grant us peace.

Mass in B Minor

Kyrie

12

20

29

33

37

41

45

49

53

57

61

65

69

73

78

82

86

102

106

110

114

118

122

61

64

67

70

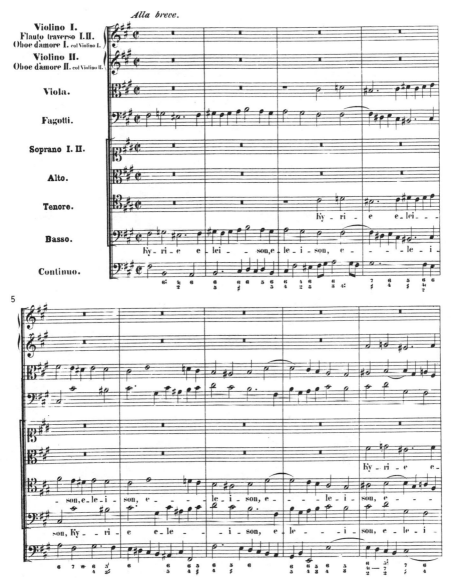

40

45

Gloria

45

8

53
- sis, in ex cel - - - - - sis, glo - - ri - a, glo - -
- sis, in ex - cel - sis, in ex - cel - sis De - - o, glo -
in ex - cel - - - - - - - - sis, glo - ri - a in ex - cel - sis De - o, in ex -
- - - - - - - - - - - sis, glo - ri - a in ex - cel - sis
o, in ex - cel - sis De - - o, glo - - ri - a. in ex - cel - sis De - o,

62

71

80

89

98

105
ter_ra pax___ ho_mi_ _ni_bus, et in ter_ra pax, in ter_ra pax,
ter_ra pax, pax ho_ mi_ni_bus, et in ter_ra pax, in ter_ra pax,
ter_ra pax, in ter_ra pax ho_ mi_nibus, et in ter_ra pax, pax, et in ter_ra pax, et
___ et in ter_ra pax ho_ mi_ ni_ bus, et in ter_ra pax, pax, et in ter_ra pax,
___ et___ in ter_ra pax,___ et in ter_ _ra

111

115

121

125

129

133

137

141

146

150

154

157

161

169

173

82

6

20

24

28

DUETTO.

92

110

16

san _ ctus,   tu so _ lus   sanctus, tu so _   lus Do _   mi _ nus,   tu solus san _

22

_ ctus, tu so _ lus Do _ _ _ _ _ _ _ _ minus, tu so _

27

lus, so _ lus Domi _ nus,   tu so _ lus   sanctus,   tu so _ lus   Dominus;

tis_si_mus, tu so _ lus al _ tis_si_mus Je _ _ _ su Chri _ ste,

Je _ _ _ _ _ su Chri _ ste, Je _ su Chri _ ste; quo _ ni _

am tu so _ _ _ lus san _ ctus, tu so _ _ lus, tu so _ lus Do _ mi _

minus, tu so _ lus al _ tis _ _ si _ mus Je _ su Chri _ ste.

124

20

24

28

41

46

51

56

60

65

70

75

84

88

92

96

104

108

112

116

120

124

Credo [Symbolum Nicenum]

158

7

14

21

28

49

cto — — rem coe — li et ter — rae, vi — si — bi — lium o — — — — —

cto — — rem coe — li et ter — rae, vi — si — bi — li — um et in — visi — bi — — li

tem, fa — ctorem coe — li et ter — — rae, fa — cto — — rem coe — li et ter —

in u — num Deum, Patrem o — mnipo — ten — tem, facto — rem coe — li et ter — rae, coe —

56

63

170

16

19

52

ro genitum, non fa _ ctum, con_sub-stanti_alem Pa _ _ _ _ tri, per quem o_mnia fa_cta

tum, non fa _ ctum, con.substanti _ a_lem Pa _ _ _ _ tri, per quem omnia fa _ _ cta

56

sunt, De_um verum de De_o ve _ ro, de De _ o ve _ _ ro,

sunt, De_um verum de De_o ve _ ro, de De _ o ve _ _ ro,

per quem o _ _ mni _ a fa _ cta, fa _ cta sunt;

per quem o _ _ mni _ a fa _ cta sunt;

qui propter nos ho _ _ mi _ nes et propter nostram sa _

qui propter nos ho _ _ mi _ nes et propter nostram sa _ lu _ tem, propter

181

184

188

10

15
re - xit, resur - re - - - - - - xit ter - ti - a di - e, re-sur-re-xit ter-ti-a
re - xit, resur - re - - - - - - xit ter - ti - a di - e, resur-rexit ter-ti-a
re - xit, resur - re - - - - - xit ter - ti - a di - e, et resur - re - xit ter-ti-a
re - xit, resur - re - - - - - xit ter - ti-a di - e, re - sur - re - xit ter-ti-a
re - xit, resur - re - - - - - xit ter - ti-a di-e, et resur - re - xit ter-ti-a

20

25

re -

re -

rexit ter_ti_a   di_e, ter_ti_a   di_e, re _ sur _ re _ _ xit, resur _ re _ xit,

rexit ter _ _ _ ti a di _ _ e, re _ sur _ rexit, re _ sur _ rexit ter_ti_a

rexit ter_ti_a   di_e, ter_ti_a   di _ _ e, re _ sur _ re _ _ xit, resur_ re _ xit

30

35

40

45

50

55

65

75

rum ventu_rus est cum glo_ri_a, ven_tu_rus est cum glo   _   ri_a, cum glori _ a   ju_di_ca_

80

85

95

100

105

116

121

126

214

que proce _ dit;

qui cum Pa _ _ tre et Fi _ li _ o simul a _ do _ ra _ tur, a _ do _

ra _ _ _ _ _ tur et con _ glo _ ri _ fi _ ca _

72

_ _ _ tur, et con_glo_ ri _ fi_ca _ tur;

78

qui lo_cu_tus est per Pro_ phe _ _ tas, lo_cu_tus est per Pro_ phe_tas, per Pro_

84

phetas lo_cu_ tus est, lo_cu_ tus est per Prophe _ _ tas, lo _cu_tus est per Pro_

90

phe _ _ tas, per Pro_phe _ tas. Et unam sanctam catholicam et a_po_sto_ li_

96

cam ec_cle _ _ _ si_am,

102

et unam sanctam catholicam et a_po_sto_li_

108

cam ec_cle_si _ am,   et unam san_ctam   ca_tho _ _ _ _

114

_ li_cam et a _ po _ sto_li_cam ec _ cle _ _ _

120

126

132

138

24
nem pecca to rum, in re missi o nem pec ca to rum, con
rum, in re missi onem pec ca to rum, in re
pec ca to rum, in remis si o nem pecca to rum, pec ca to
rum, in re mis si o nem pec ca to rum, pec ca to
in re missi o nem pecca to rum, in re missi onem pec ca to
32
fi te or, con fi te or u num ba pti sma in re mis si o nem pecca
missi o nem pecca to rum, con fi te or, con fi
rum, in re missi o nem pecca to rum, con fi te or u num ba
rum, con fi te or, con fi te or u num ba pti sma, u
rum,
40
to rum, pecca to rum, in re missi o nem pecca
te or u num ba ptisma, con fi te or u num ba pti sma, con fi te
pti sma, u num ba pti sma in re missi o nem pecca to rum, con fi te or u num ba
num bapti sma, con fi te or, con fi te or u num bapti sma,
con fi te or, con fi te or u num ba pti sma in re

72
to - - - rum, in re - missi - o - - nem pecca - to - - - - rum, pec - - ca - to - - - -
pec - ca - to - rum, con - fi - te - or u - num ba - pti - sma, con - fi - - te -
- ca - to - rum, con - - fi - te - or u - num ba - pti - - -
to - - - rum, in re - mis - si - o - - nem pecca - to - rum, in -
con - - fi - te - or u - num ba - pti - - sma
80
rum, con - fi - - te - or, con - fi - - - te - or u - num ba - ptisma
or unum ba - pti - sma, con - fi - - te - or, con - fi - te - or u - - num ba - pti - -
sma in re - mis - si - o - nem pec - ca - to - -
re - mis - - si - o - nem pec - ca - to - - - rum, in re - missi - o - - nem pecca - to - -
in re - mis - si - o - nem pec - ca - to - - rum,
88
in remissi - o - - - nem pec - - ca - to - rum, in re - missi - o - - nem pecca -
sma, con - fi - te - or, in re - mis - si - o - - nem pec - - - ca - torum, con -
rum, con - fi - te - or u - num ba - pti - - - sma in re - missi - o - - nem pecca - to - rum,
rum, con - - - - fi - - - te - - -
in re - missi - o - - nem pecca - to - - - rum,

121
Adagio.
to - rum. Et ex - pe - cto, ex - pe - cto
to - rum. Et ex - pe - cto, ex - pe - cto re -
pec - ca - to - rum. Et ex - pe - cto. ex - pecto resur - re - cti -
pec - ca - to - rum. Et ex - pe - cto, ex - pecto resur - re - cti -
to - rum. Et ex - pe - cto, ex - pe -
130
re - sur - re - cti - o - nem mortu - o - rum, ex -
sur - re - cti - o - nem mor - tu - o - rum,
o - nem mor - tu - o - rum, mor - tu - o - rum, mor - tu - o - rum,
o - nem mor - tu - o - rum, re - sur - re - cti - onem mortu - o - rum,
cto re - surre - cti - onem mortu - o - rum,
138
pe - cto re - sur - re - cti - o - nem mor - tu - o -
ex - pe - cto, ex - pe - cto re - sur - re - cti - o - nem mortu - o -
ex - pe - cto resur - re - cti - o - nem mortu - o -
ex - pe - cto resur - re - cti - onem mor - tu - o -
ex - pe - cto resur - re - cti - o - nem mortu - o -

37
pe - cto, ex - pe-cto re-sur - re - - cti - o-nem mortu - o - - - - rum, re-sur-
- - cto, ex - pe-cto re - sur-re-cti - o-nem mortu - o - - - rum,
pe - - - cto re-sur - re - - cti - o - nem, re-sur - re-cti - o - - - -
cto, ex-pe - - cto re-sur - re - - cti - o-nem mortu - o - - - rum,
cto, ex-pe - cto re - - sur - re-cti - o - - nem mortu - o - - - - rum,

44

51

58

72

79

86

93
men, A - men, A - men, Amen, A - men,
men, A - men, A - men, A
A - men, A - men, A
A - men, A
A - men, A - men

100

Sanctus

8

20
- - - ctus, san - - - - - - - - - - ctus, sanctus Do - minus De -
- - - ctus, san - - - - - - - - - - ctus, san - ctus Do - minus
- - - ctus, san - - - - - - - - - - ctus, san - ctus Do - minus De -
- - - ctus, san - - - - - - - - - - ctus, san - - - - - -
- - - ctus, san - - - - - - - - - - ctus, san - ctus Do - minus
De - us Sa - baoth, san - ctus Do - minus De - us Sa - baoth, san - ctus Do - minus

32

44

48

56

88

145

153

161

Osanna and Benedictus

268

25
- na in ex - cel - - - - - - sis, o - san - - - - - na, o - san - -
- sis, o - san - - - na in ex - cel - sis, o - sanna, o - san - - - na, o - san - -
- - - - - - na in ex - cel - sis, o - sanna, o - san - - - na, o - san - -
- na in ex - cel - - - - - - sis, o - sanna, o - san - - - - - - na, o -
o - sanna in ex - cel - sis, o - sanna in ex - cel - sis,
o - sanna in ex - cel - sis, o - sanna in ex - cel - sis,
o - sanna in ex - cel - sis, o - sanna in ex - cel - sis,
o - sanna in ex - cel - sis, o - sanna in ex - cel - sis,

33
- na in ex - cel - - - - - - sis, o - san - - - - - - - - na, o -
- na in ex - cel - - - - - - sis, o - san - na, o - san - - - - - - na, o -
- na in ex - cel - - - - - - sis, o - san - na, o - sanna in ex - cel - - - sis, o -
sanna in ex - cel - - - - - sis, o - san - na, o - san - - - na in ex - cel - sis, o -
o - san - na in ex - cel - sis,
o - san - na in ex - cel - sis, o -
o - san - na in ex - cel - sis, o - san - - - - -
o - san - na in ex - cel - sis,

41

57

73
na, o - sanna in ex - cel - sis, o - sanna in ex - cel - sis, o -
sanna in ex - cel - sis, o - sanna in ex - cel - sis, o - sanna in ex - cel - sis, o -
o - sanna in ex - cel - sis, o - sanna in ex - cel - sis, o -
cel - sis, o - sanna in ex - cel - sis, o -
na in ex - cel - sis, o - san - na, o - san - na in ex - cel - sis,
san - na, o - san - na in ex - cel - sis,
o - san - na in ex - cel - sis,
o - san - na in ex - cel - sis, o -

81

89
tr
tr
o - sanna in ex - cel - - - sis, o - san - - - - na in ex - cel_sis, o -
o - sanna in ex - cel - - sis, o - sanna in ex - cel_sis,
o - sanna in ex - cel - - - sis, o - sanna in ex - cel_sis,
o - sanna in ex - cel - - - sis, o - sanna in ex - cel_sis,
- sis, o - sanna in ex - cel - sis, o - san - - - na in ex - cel_sis,
- sis, o - sanna in ex - cel - sis, o - sanna, o - sanna, o -
- sis, o - sanna in ex - cel - sis, o - sanna, o - sanna, o -
- sis, o - sanna in ex - cel - sis, o - sanna, o - sanna, o -

97

105
tr
forte
piano
sanna in ex - cel - sis, o - san - na, o - sanna, o -
sanna in ex - cel - sis, o - san - na, o - sanna, o -
san - na, o - san - na, o - sanna, o - sanna, o -
o - sanna in ex - cel - sis, o - san - na, o -
o - sanna in ex - cel - sis, o - san - na, o - san - na,
o - sanna in ex - cel - sis, o - san - na, o - sanna,
o - san - na, o - san - na, o - sanna,
o - sanna in ex - cel - sis, o - san - na,

113

forte
sanna in ex - cel - - sis.
forte
sanna in ex - cel - - sis.
forte
sanna in ex - cel - - sis.
forte
sanna in ex - cel - - sis.
piano forte
o - sanna in ex - cel - - sis.
piano forte
o - sanna in ex - cel - - sis.
piano forte
o - sanna in ex - cel - - sis.
piano forte
o - sanna in ex - cel - - sis.
forte

122

131

140

Do _ mi _ ni, qui ve _ nit, be _ ne di _ ctus qui ve _ nit, qui

ve _ nit in no _ mine Do _ mi _ ni, in no _ _ mine Do _ mi _ ni, be _ ne

di _ ctus, be _ ne _ di _ _ ctus qui ve _ nit in no _ mine Do _ mi _

ni.

Be _

32

35

38

41

44

ve_nit in no_mine Do_mi_ni, qui ve_ _ _ _ nit,   qui   ve_nit in

47

no_ _ mine Do_mi_ni.

51

54

Osanna da Capo.

Agnus Dei

290

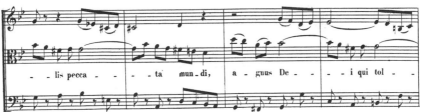

33

_ _ lis pecca _ _ ta, qui tollis pec _ ca _ ta, pecca _ _ ta mun_di, qui tol _ _ lis pec

37

ca_ta, mi _ se _ re _ re, qui tol _ lis pec_ca_ta, mi _ se _ re _ re no _ bis, mi _ se.re

41

_ _ re no _ bis, mi _ se_re_re no _ bis, mi _ se _ re _ re nobis, mise_re_re no_

45

bis.

293

14

19

23

27

32

37

41

Fine.

Appendix:
"Et in unum Dominum" (p. 170), alternative vocal parts

END OF EDITION